Language Arts

Super-creative Art Activities That Build Language Arts Skills and Engage Kids of All Learning Styles

BY KATHI HUDSON & JOANNE IVINS

NEW YORK • TORONTO • LONDON • AUCKLAND • SYDNEY
MEXICO CITY • NEW DELHI • HONG KONG

*We are grateful to the many people who have
influenced our teaching throughout the years.
We are also indebted to our families
(Joanne's husband Larry, my children, Jessica
and Josh, and my editing sister, Diane)
for their support, encouragement and help
as we struggled to put these ideas to paper
in a way that we hope will inspire enthusiasm
in teaching and learning.*

No part of this publication may be reproduced in whole or in part, or stored in a retrieval system, or transmitted in any form or by any means, electronic, mechanical, photocopying, recording, or otherwise, without written permission of the publisher. For information regarding permission write to Scholastic Professional Books, 555 Broadway, New York, NY 10012.

Cover and interior design by Kathy Massaro
Interior art by James G. Hale
Student artwork by students of North Wayne Elementary School

ISBN: 0-590-00488-3

Copyright © 1998 by Kathi Hudson and Joanne Ivins. All rights reserved. Printed in the U.S.A

Contents

Introduction 5
    What You'll Need 5
    How the Activities Are Organized 5

Story Elements

    Story Cut-Aparts 7
    Story Detail Viewfinder 9
    Setting/Character Picture Frames 11
    Setting/Character Dioramas 13
    Prediction Cards 15

Parts of Speech

    Acting-Verb Cartoons 17
    Pictonoun Paragraphs 19
    Helping-Verb Hands & Linking-Verb Chains 22
    Adjective Pictures 24
    Conjunction Junction 26
    Impressive Possessive Portraits 28
    Preposition Scenes 31
    Homophone Cubes 34
    Animated Adverbs 36
    Antonym & Synonym Puzzle Pieces 38

Reading Skills

    Main-Idea Flowerpot 40
    Nonfiction Kites 43
    Story Ads 45

Story Genre Paintings 47

Cause-and-Effect Inventions 49

Double-Meaning Scenes 51

Past-Tense Silhouettes 53

Cartoon Quotations 55

Base-Word House 57

Word-Root Trees 59

Spelling Skills

Illustrated Definitions 61

Rough-Tough Words 63

Palindrome Pictures 65

Handwriting Skills

Capital-Idea Pictures 67

Painted Quotations 69

Signature Silhouettes 71

Good Signs 73

Poetry

Paper-Animal Haiku 75

Cartoon Limerick Strips 77

Color-Coded Poems 79

Introduction

Language arts skills help lay the foundation of all verbal learning. So we teachers agree that students' ability to comprehend and communicate figures heavily in their success across the curriculum. Engaging your language arts learners in a kinesthetic and creative way is crucial. That's why Joanne, an art teacher, and I, a language arts teacher, collaborated on this book. We believe that the easy-to-do activities in this book will help you meet this challenge. In fact, we're excited by the progress we've already seen with students of all learning styles in reading and writing skills ranging from poetry to punctuation.

Making art clearly benefits students on many levels. First, it gives them the chance to learn creatively, literally having a hand in the process. Second, artwork engages students by engaging their senses: The colors and design of a well-devised project, the feel and even the smell of the materials, the manipulation of these materials toward a tangible creation, and the inevitable feedback of peers and parents all come together to reach students of all learning styles and strengths. Finally, art making builds students' confidence and self-esteem by offering them the freedom to execute their own ideas, decisions, and evaluations—without the risk of being "wrong." And perhaps most important, it's fun!

What You'll Need

In addition to your students' imagination and enthusiasm the activities in this book require very little in the way of materials to complete. Besides students' pencils and notebooks, most projects require only construction paper, safety scissors, markers or crayons, and glue. The few exceptions require the use of things like index cards, paints, and pastels. In addition to these basic materials, you'll see the occasional cardboard paper towel tube (activity 33—Paper-Animal Haiku) or shoe box (activity 4—Setting/Character Dioramas). For these, we often suggest that you ask students to bring the material from home—or, where possible, we offer easy-to-find alternatives.

How the Activities Are Organized

To make them even more doable, the activities are structured so that you can see the important elements at a glance. Each activity is organized in the following way:

SKILLS HEADING This box at the top of the page lets you know what Language Arts element the activity addresses. These include Story Elements, Parts of Speech, Reading, Spelling, Handwriting, and Poetry.

OVERVIEW The overview lets you know what students will be creating and what language arts skill they will be honing along the way.

MATERIALS Materials are listed on a per-student basis—that is, just one of each material shown unless otherwise noted. The amount of scrap paper, crayons, markers, and other collective materials is determined by what kids need, what is available, and your judgment.

ADVANCE PREPARATION Some activities require advanced preparation. In most cases the activities call for you to precut paper or bring in magazines or a library book. In a few instances it will be necessary to model the activity for students before they do it themselves.

GETTING STARTED This section helps you frame the activity within the context of a lesson plan. It helps you focus the class on the language arts skill the activity addresses and quickly lays out any brainstorming or discussing you and your students may need to do.

WHAT TO DO These simple steps show you how to instruct students in doing the activity.

EXTENDED LEARNING This section offers interesting variations on the activity, often providing a way of modifying the activity to give it a cross-curricular link to subjects like science and social studies.

WAYS TO SHARE This feature suggests ways of exhibiting your students' artwork.

As lifelong learners, Joanne and I are excited about this new twist in our teaching strategies. We hope these activities will delight your students as much as they have delighted ours. In addition to offering vibrant and interesting art experiences, they'll help you provide students with valuable practice in a variety of language arts skills. You need only select an activity and watch students build their language skills as they enjoy the fun of making art.

Kathi Hudson   *Joanne Quins*

 Story Elements

Story Cut-Aparts

Overview

Students create and cut apart symbols of a story, then fill the spaces with story details to help them analyze a favorite book.

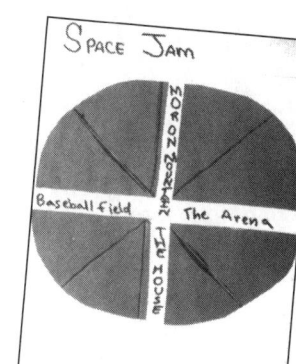

Materials

- 9" x 12" construction paper, white and another color (1 sheet of each per student)
- pencil
- notebook paper
- scissors
- glue
- fine-point marker

Getting Started

Invite students to briefly summarize their story and to think of a shape or an object that helps them remember the story's theme. For example, they might choose to illustrate a peach for *James and the Giant Peach*, a train for *The Boxcar Children*, or—as shown here—a heart for *Secret Boyfriend*. Then explain that they will cut up the object, pull it apart, and insert the story's main ideas within it.

What to Do

1 Ask students to sketch on colored construction paper the shape they've chosen, making it large enough to fill most of the paper.

2 Instruct students to write the main points of the story in four or five short sentences on a sheet of notebook paper.

7

Story Elements

3 Show students how to draw lines to divide the shape into sections for each main point they've listed.

4 Using the lines as a guide, students can cut the shape into pieces. Then invite them to reassemble the shape by gluing the colored pieces onto the white construction paper, leaving about a one-inch space between the pieces.

5 Ask students to reread their sentences to make sure they're clear and that there are no spelling or grammatical errors. Once they've done this, invite them to use a fine-point marker to write the sentences in the cut-aparts' spaces.

6 To complete the project, ask students to write the story's title at the top of the page or around the outside of the shape.

Extended Learning

Invite students to use this activity to review a magazine or newspaper article or any other nonfiction selection. You might also suggest that they use Story Cut-Aparts as part of an oral book report.

Ways to Share

- Compile students' Story Cut-Aparts into a class book that can be shared with other classes or used to demonstrate how various people can read the same story and view it differently.

- Have students save some of their Story Cut-Aparts throughout the year in their assessment portfolios. At the end of the year, bind them together to make a personal book for each student.

- Use Story Cut-Aparts to make a classroom display by arranging them on a bulletin board or blank wall.

▲▲▲▲▲▲▲▲▲▲▲▲▲▲▲▲▲▲▲▲▲▲▲▲▲▲▲▲▲▲ **Story Elements**

Story Detail Viewfinder

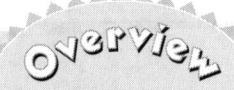

Students make viewfinders to demonstrate reading comprehension skills such as noting details and making predictions.

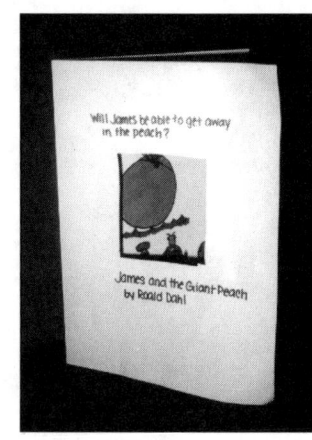

Materials

- 1 sheet of 9" x 12" white construction paper
- ruler
- pencil
- scissors
- crayons or markers
- pen or fine-point marker

Getting Started

Once students have chosen a story to focus on, discuss how story details augment and enrich the meaning of the story. Explain that the details often give important clues to what will happen next or to how the story will end. Ask students to write a brief summary of the selection, listing important details of the story.

What to Do

1 Ask students to fold the construction paper in half like a greeting card.

2 Instruct students to use a ruler and pencil to draw a rectangular or square box on the front cover of the card. Then ask them to cut out the box to create a window.

9

Story Elements

3 Have students open their viewfinder card and illustrate the story details on the right-hand side. You may want to suggest that they close the card occasionally to be sure that the viewfinder only reveals a few details without giving the ending away.

4 Ask students to use a pen or fine-point marker to write a question above the window on the front of the card. The question should invite the reader to predict what will happen from the detail(s) they can see inside the window. If a student had read *James and the Giant Peach*, he might ask, "Will James be able to get away in the peach?"

5 On the back of the card, ask students to write the story title, author, and a brief, detail-rich summary—including how the story ends.

Extended Learning

Students might enjoy making an oversized viewfinder. Invite students to illustrate an unfolded sheet of construction paper with story details. Then ask them to make a viewfinder by cutting out a window from a 4-by-6-inch index card. Invite students to move the viewfinder over the paper to view and list as many story details as possible.

Ways to Share

- Encourage students to share their viewfinders with their classmates and friends. Were they able to answer the questions and predict the story's ending?

- Display Story Detail Viewfinders in the hallway, cafeteria, or auditorium to encourage other students to read the story and look for details.

Story Elements

ACTIVITY 3

Setting/Character Picture Frames

Students create picture frames that focus on character and setting and provide you with a fresh and colorful way to assess their story comprehension.

Materials

- 1 sheet of 12" x 18" black or dark-colored construction paper
- ruler
- pencil
- 11" x 17" drawing paper
- crayons
- pastels
- watercolor paints
- scissors
- glue
- **Optional:** collage materials such as glitter, dried flowers, textile scraps, pipe cleaners, and string

Advance Preparation

If you don't have 11-by-17-inch drawing paper on hand, precut larger sheets to those dimensions.

Getting Started

After reading a story or book in class, invite students to brainstorm a list of setting details and characters. In *Charlotte's Web*, for example, setting details would include "fields," "barn," and "pigpen." Then ask students to list characters by name (proper noun) and by common noun—for example, "Jeffrey Goose." For each common noun, ask students to supply an adjective (from story details or clues) that describes the character, such as "*nice* spider" or "*wandering* rat."

11

Story Elements

What to Do

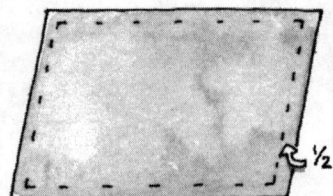

1 Ask students to hold the construction paper horizontally. Then have them use the ruler to measure a half inch from each edge of the construction paper at the corners. Ask them to make light pencil marks there. Then put the paper aside.

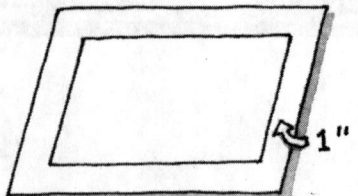

2 On the 11-by-17-inch drawing paper, ask students to make another frame, this time one inch from each edge. Have them draw the entire frame on this paper.

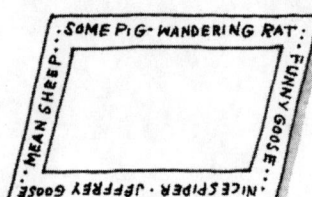

3 Invite students to use capital letters to print an adjective and a common noun for each character in the story outside the frame. These word pairs should be spaced evenly around the frame of the picture and traced in crayon. (Students may want to draw dots or other small shapes to separate word pairs.)

4 Invite students to draw the story setting inside the frame using pastels. Encourage them to include as many setting details as possible.

5 Give students another sheet of drawing paper, and ask them to draw the characters of the story in crayon or paint. Then ask students to cut out the characters and glue them to the appropriate places on the setting.

6 When students have completed the setting and character picture, they can glue it to the dark construction paper, placing the corners of the picture on the pencil marks they made in step 1.

Extended Learning

Use this activity to dress up a more traditional book report. The Setting/Character Picture Frame could be used as a cover for the book report. For a social studies connection, have students use art to highlight important places and people in history.

Ways to Share

- Display Setting/Character Picture Frames of award-winning books or stories on hallway walls or the library bulletin board.

 Story Elements

ACTIVITY 4

Setting/Character Dioramas

Students create 3-D environments and their inhabitants to actively learn about the essential story elements of setting, plot, and character.

Materials

- shoe box or other small box
- crayons or markers
- glue
- construction paper scraps, wallpaper samples, fabric swatches
- pencil
- drawing paper
- scissors

Advance Preparation

Ask each student to bring a shoe box or small box of comparable size from home. Gather a few extras in case some students can't supply their own.

Getting Started

After reading a story or book in class, ask students to list its characters and setting details. *The Secret Garden*, for example, should include plants and grass, along with the children who take refuge there. Explain to students that they will be constructing a small scene from the selection that includes the things they have read about in the story.

What to Do

1. Invite students to use crayons and markers, scrap paper, wallpaper, and fabric to illustrate the inside of the shoe box with setting details. Encourage them to decorate the bottom (floor or ground), the sides (walls of a room or outdoor scenery), and the top (ceiling or sky). They may add details to the outside of the box too.

13

Story Elements

2 On drawing paper, students can draw, color, and cut out small figures to represent the different characters. When cutting the characters out, students should leave about a 1/4-inch margin of paper at the bottom of each figure.

3 Show students how to fold this extra paper back and glue it down to the floor or ground of their dioramas to make their characters stand.

4 Invite students to create and cut out other items that represent details in the setting. To monitor comprehension, check that everything students add comes from the story.

5 Each student should write the title and author of the story on the side or top of the diorama along with her or his name.

Extended Learning

Setting/Character Dioramas can bring the excitement of active learning to other areas of the curriculum. For instance, students could respond to a science lesson on an inventor by portraying the figure in a setting that shows his or her invention and its current applications. Or students might portray a historical figure in an important setting (for example, Dr. Martin Luther King, Jr., delivering his "I Have a Dream" speech in Washington, D.C.).

Ways to Share

- Display these dioramas on a table or the top of a bookshelf, and invite students and family members to view the work.

- Select a story or historical event that lends itself to a before-and-after view, such as the first moon landing. Students can work in pairs to create two scenes that illustrate the effects of the event. Staple the dioramas together to highlight the impact, and display it for other classes to view.

- Divide the class into small groups and invite each group to create three dioramas that illustrate the beginning, middle, and end of a book. Each group might work on a different book. When these three-part tableaux are completed, a volunteer from each group can present the display to the class.

Story Elements

ACTIVITY 5

Prediction Cards

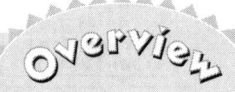

Prediction Cards combine the fun of guessing with the joy of making art. Students use details from the beginning of a story to encourage classmates to predict what will happen and to inspire them to read the story themselves. The activity helps to emphasize the importance of prediction as a reading strategy.

Materials

- 1 sheet of 9" x 18" white or light-colored construction paper
- pencil
- crayons, markers, or colored pencils
- ruler
- pen or fine-point marker

Getting Started

Select two stories that offer surprise (or at least interesting) endings. Then divide the class in half and assign one story to each group. Ask students to read and summarize their story. Once students are ready to summarize, remind them that it helps to divide the story into a beginning, a middle, and an end, listing important events that occur in each part. Ask them to do this quietly so they don't give away the ending.

What to Do

1. Show students how to make a large paper card by folding the construction paper in half horizontally.

2. Ask students to use crayons, markers, or colored pencils to illustrate the front of the card (in the center) with one or more details from the story. The picture should be no more than three to four inches high.

15

Story Elements

3 Above the illustration, ask students to use a ruler and pencil to lightly draw several handwriting guidelines (about 3/4-inch to 1 inch apart). Then, at the bottom of the page, have them use the ruler to lightly pencil in a rectangle approximately three by eight inches. (This is where they will write their prediction question.)

4 Invite students to write a sentence or a short paragraph about the beginning of the story in the space at the top of the page in pen. Inside the rectangle at the bottom, students can write a prediction question that challenges the reader to guess the ending of the story.

5 Inside the paper card, ask students to draw and color a detailed picture of the end of the story. Explain that the reader should be able to tell from looking at the picture how the story ends and whether their prediction is correct.

6 Ask students to write a sentence or paragraph about how the story ends on the back of the card.

Extended Learning

Try this activity with smaller groups and several different stories, assigning a different book to each group. You can also use Prediction Cards to have students illustrate and predict an event in history or to show a cause-and-effect relationship in science.

Ways to Share

- Share Prediction Cards with another class that is about to read the same story. Remind them that they should view only the front of the card before reading. They can read the rest of the card when they finish the story—and check to see how their predictions turned out!

- Display Prediction Cards in the hallway or in another communal area to spark the reading curiosity of other students.

Parts of Speech

ACTIVITY 6

Acting-Verb Cartoons

Students animate and personify language to increase their understanding of action verbs.

Materials

- drawing paper
- pencil
- crayons or markers
- dictionary

Optional (see Extended Learning, page 18):
- construction paper in a variety of colors
- construction paper scraps
- scissors
- glue

Advance Preparation

You might want to practice animating some action verbs so you can model the activity more effectively for your students. Simply take a verb like *bounce*, for example, and bring the letters to life by pasting them to the page as if they were actually bouncing.

Getting Started

Review the main parts of speech with students, focusing on action verbs. Have students work as a class to brainstorm a list of action verbs and write them on the chalkboard. Make sure dictionaries are available for students to check their words. After they have developed a list of 20–30 action verbs, divide the class into small groups or pairs.

17

Parts of Speech

What to Do

1 Share your Acting-Verb Cartoon with the class, and then work with your students to create another cartoon on the chalkboard. For example:

The letters in the word *run* have legs and look as if they are running.
The p in *slip* seems to be slipping down away from the other letters.
The e in *dive* looks like it's diving into the water.

2 Ask the members of each group or pair to work together to create a few Acting-Verb Cartoons of their own.

3 After students have sketched each verb cartoon in pencil, invite them to use crayons or markers to add color and width to the letters.

Extended Learning

Invite students to illustrate action verbs by sketching a figure or a simple object in motion that contains the word itself. To illustrate *drive*, for example, students might make a simple line drawing of a car, leaving out details within the outline. Then they could fill that space with bubble letters that spell the word *drive* and fit snugly inside the outline of the picture.

Students can also make Acting-Verb Cartoons from construction paper. Ask them to cut the letters of their verb from scraps and glue them to construction paper of a different color. Invite students to use additional scraps to draw and cut out a shape or figure that illustrates the verb. Then ask them to glue the shape to the paper near the letters of the verb.

Ways to Share

- Use Acting-Verb Cartoons to make a great display for the wall of the gym.

- Encourage students to combine their Acting-Verb Cartoons to form a class book.

Parts of Speech

Pictonoun Paragraphs

Overview

To enhance grammar skills and increase vocabulary, students write a brief story or paragraph, replacing the nouns with their own flip-up illustrations.

Materials

- notebook paper or scrap paper
- chart paper
- ruler
- scissors
- index cards (2 or 3 per student)
- pencil
- colored pencils
- glue
- 1 sheet of 9" x 18" white construction paper

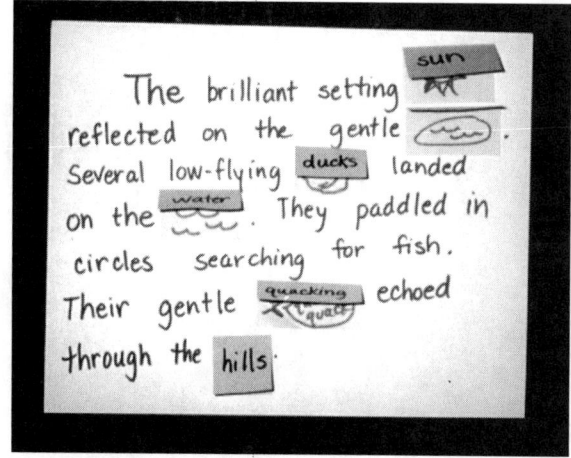

Advance Preparation

- Give each student two or three index cards folded in half.

- Write a short paragraph with the class on a large sheet of chart paper. Be sure to leave sufficient space to display students' pictonouns.

- Read through the finished paragraph with the class, marking each noun students identify.

- Divide the class into groups of four, and assign a noun or two to each group. Ask group members to work together to illustrate each noun on the inside of their cards. Ask them to write the noun on the front.

- When groups are done, glue the pictonouns to the paragraph in the correct places so students can see how it's done. Then read the story aloud, flipping up the pictonouns as you go.

Parts of Speech

Getting Started

Work with the class to brainstorm a list of 15–20 nouns. Take the opportunity to build vocabulary by introducing new words for students to familiarize themselves with. Remember that the nouns you choose should be fairly easy to illustrate. When your list is complete, ask students to sketch some of the nouns on notebook or scrap paper.

What to Do

1 Have students create their own paragraphs incorporating some of the nouns from your list.

2 On the construction paper, show students how to measure and lightly draw double-spaced lines to accommodate their story.

3 Invite students to write their story on the construction paper, leaving sufficient space between words and lines for the pictonouns.

4 Ask students to identify the nouns in their story or paragraph by underlining them.

Parts of Speech

5 Now show students how to cut the index card into 9 equal parts. After cutting, they can fold each part in half. Explain that they should print each noun on the outside of each card and illustrate it on the inside.

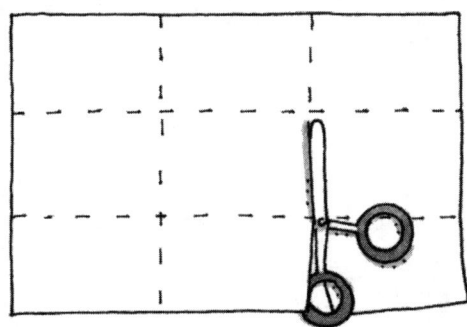

6 Invite students to glue the completed pictonouns to the appropriate noun in their story or paragraph. Then ask them to share their story with a neighbor. Have partners check the illustrations to make sure they correctly define the nouns.

Extended Learning

You might want to use pictonouns as a cooperative-learning activity, with each group completing a paragraph on chart paper. Or have students use the activity to enliven a social studies or science paragraph.

Ways to Share

◉ Students can present their Pictonoun Paragraphs to other students in your class or school. Have the audience read the story and then write definitions of the pictonouns, based on the illustrations and their context.

Parts of Speech

Helping-Verb Hands & Linking-Verb Chains

Overview

Students make cutout hands and paper chains to learn about helping verbs and linking verbs. The hands and links provide visual metaphors for the functions of these essential parts of speech.

Materials

- 9" x 12" construction paper in a variety of skin colors (one sheet per student)
- 2" x 9" strips of red construction paper (one per student)
- pencil
- scissors
- fine-point black marker or black pen
- glue

Advance Preparation

Precut the red construction paper into 2-by-9-inch strips, one per student.

Getting Started

Review verbs, discussing how most verbs—action verbs—show action. Model some sample sentences that use action verbs. Then explain that helping verbs and linking verbs do not show action. You might point out that helping verbs work together with action verbs or main verbs. Examples include "*had* run," "*does* play," and "*may* leave." For linking verbs, you might explain that they link a subject with a noun, pronoun, or adjective, as in the following sentences: "The answer *is* seven." "The winner *could* be me." "The pizza *tasted* funny." Work with students to create lists of helping verbs and linking verbs.

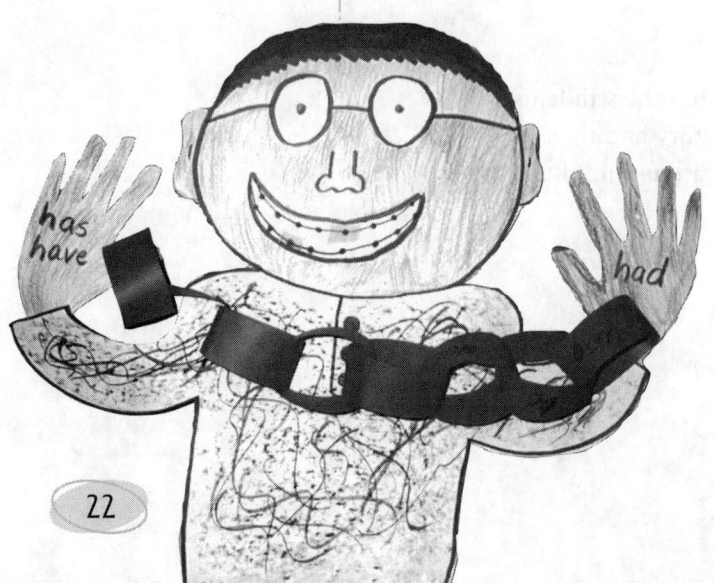

22

Parts of Speech

What to Do

1 Invite students to trace their hand on a sheet of construction paper and cut it out. Then ask them to print a helping verb on each finger of the cutout hand in an order that is easy for them to remember—for example, alphabetical order, as in the picture to the right.

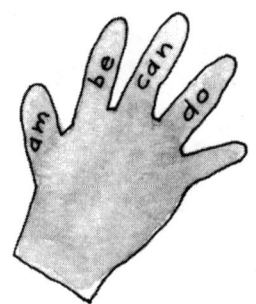

2 Now work with the class on the list of linking verbs (*am, is, are,* and *were,* along with others, such as *seem, taste, appear,* and *remain*. Have students print each of these linking verbs in the center of a red strip of construction paper.

3 Invite students to paste the links together to create a paper chain. Then have them attach the chain to Helping-Verb Hands, as shown.

4 As a wrap-up, ask students to write sentences that include at least one linking verb or one helping verb. Remind them to use the hands and links as a visual reminder.

Extended Learning

Enhance this activity by inviting students to draw the torso and arms of a boy or girl. Then ask them to cut out the figures and color them with markers or crayons. When the figures are constructed, invite students to write main or action verbs on the torso.

Ways to Share

- Invite students to make Helping-Verb Hands and Linking-Verb Chains with another class as a paired sharing activity.

- Display at least one student project on a wall in the classroom as a visual reminder of helping verbs and linking verbs.

Parts of Speech

Adjective Pictures

In this activity, students create imagery by carefully selecting adjectives to fill blanks in a sentence that you present to them. Then they make adjective pictures that show the function and power of these parts of speech.

Materials

- 1 sheet of 9" x 18" white construction paper
- pencil
- crayons or markers
- dictionary
- ruler

Advance Preparation

Find a few books that feature monsters and castles.

Getting Started

- Invite children to brainstorm a list of adjectives.

- Share the books you selected, and enjoy children's fascination with the fantastic. Ask students to identify the adjectives used in the stories to describe monsters and castles. Discuss how these words create a "picture" and how adjectives modify nouns or other adjectives.

- Finally, invite students to come up with adjectives that they might use to describe a monster or a castle.

What to Do

1 Ask students to position the construction paper vertically. Then, using a ruler, they should pencil a light line 2 inches from the top and bottom of the paper. Each of these two spaces will be used to write a descriptive sentence.

24

Parts of Speech

2 In the top margin, ask students to copy this sentence (leaving ample space for each missing word):

Beware of this creature with a _____ head, _____ body, _____ tail, and _____ feet.

3 In the bottom margin, ask students to copy this sentence (again reminding them to allow sufficient space to add adjectives):

He lives in a _____ castle in the _____ forest.

4 After they've finished writing the two sentences, ask students to underline the adjective spaces in color. Then encourage them to fill the blanks with descriptive words. They may want to use their dictionaries.

5 When their sentences are complete, ask students to illustrate them.

Extended Learning

For a fun math connection, help students graph the frequency of adjectives used in the class's sentences. Work with your students to draw a bar graph that shows adjectives on the horizontal axis and the number of times they were used on the vertical axis.

Ways to Share

- Set up a classroom center for individual readings. Ask small groups to take turns at the center, with each person in the group reading their adjective picture sentences to the rest of the group. You might also want to encourage students to supply adjectives for a third sentence:

  The _____ creatures in the nearby town wear _____ clothes.

- Display students' work next to the class bar graph of frequently used adjectives.

Parts of Speech

 ACTIVITY 10

Conjunction Junction

Students manipulate sentences written on paper strips to see how a conjunction can make an interesting sentence out of two less interesting ones.

Materials

- notebook paper
- 1" x 9" strips of light-colored construction paper (about 10 per student)
- 9" x 18" construction paper in a variety of colors (1 sheet per student)
- pencil
- fine-point marker
- colored-dot stickers (5–6 per student)
- glue
- scissors

Advance Preparation

Precut the construction paper to the dimensions shown in the Materials list.

Getting Started

Discuss combining sentences with students and how this skill makes sentences and paragraphs more interesting to read. Give students a few examples, using conjunctions and the proper punctuation. Ask students to help you list commonly used conjunctions, and then write them on the chalkboard. When the list is done, work with the class to select a writing topic such as "My Favorite Animal" or "My Favorite Sport."

What to Do

1 Ask students to write six or eight (the number should be even) short sentences about the topic on a sheet of notebook paper. After students have checked their spelling, ask them to use pencils to copy each sentence onto a construction paper strip.

Parts of Speech

2 Invite students to manipulate the strips to see which sentence pairs are most related. Explain that these pairs will combine to make the best compound sentences. Also remind them to consider which conjunction will work best.

3 Demonstrate connecting pairs of strips at 45° or 90° angles. Then invite students to connect their sentence pairs at angles that will make a nice design on the construction paper. Explain that any angle is okay, and encourage them to work on their layout until they like it. Then have students paste the sentence strips to the paper.

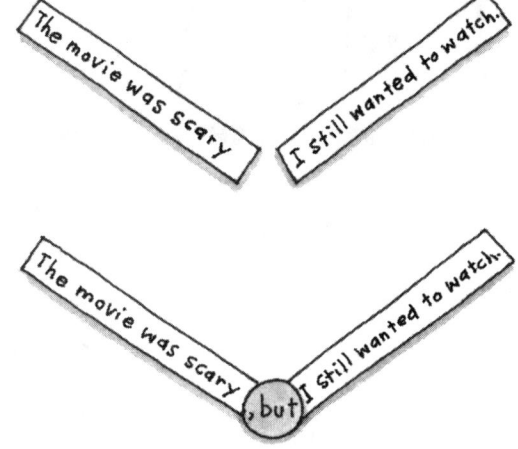

4 At the vertex of each angle, ask students to attach a circular sticker with a comma and the appropriate conjunction. When the stickers are affixed, remind students to change the first letter of the second sentence from capital to lowercase. Then suggest that they trace over the pencil with fine-point markers so the words show up well.

5 Students may add illustrations to the empty spaces on the paper. Or they could use leftover construction paper and glue to make a collage.

6 As a follow-up, ask students to copy the combined sentences onto the same notebook paper they used to write their original sentences. The resulting contrast should clearly demonstrate the benefits of combining sentences.

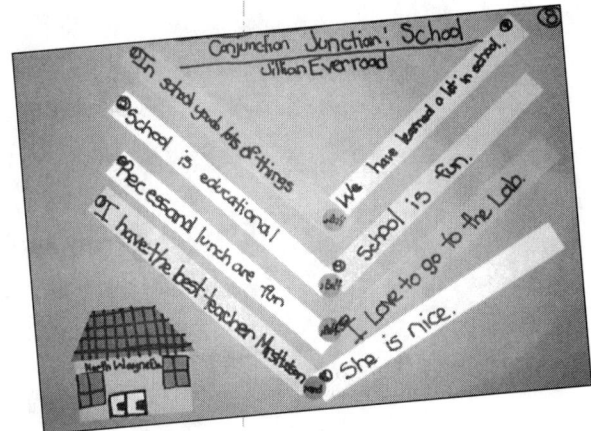

Extended Learning

Use this activity to have students describe the steps in a procedure, a recipe (for a snack that you might make in class), or a science experiment.

Ways to Share

- Conjunction Junctions might be displayed on hallway walls—with the original handwritten sentences posted beneath them.

Parts of Speech

ACTIVITY 11

Impressive Possessive Portraits

Overview

Students make portraits of someone they admire—either a historical figure, a modern leader, or a member of their family or community—to build their understanding of singular and plural possessives.

Materials

- 2 thoroughly washed plastic-foam trays
- pencil
- marker
- tempera paint (no light colors)
- brayer (small roller)
- magazines and photographs
- scissors
- glue
- 4" x 6" white construction paper (3 sheets per student)
- light-colored construction paper
    9" x 12" (1 sheet per student)
    12" x 18" (1 sheet per student)

Advance Preparation

- Ask each student to bring two plastic-foam trays from home, reminding them to wash the trays thoroughly. Collect some extras yourself.

- Precut construction paper to the dimensions listed in the Materials section.

- Ask students to start thinking about someone they admire and would like to do a portrait of. As they think of a person, they should also be collecting images from magazines or photographs that they can add to their Impressive Possessive Portraits.

28

Parts of Speech

Getting Started

Review possessives with students, and then guide them in brainstorming a list of singular and plural cases. You might want to begin by having them write about things that belong to them. When they finish a brief list, ask them to express the terms in generic possessives—for example "boy's game" or "girl's bike." Once students have a firm understanding of possessives, ask them to share the name of the person they most admire.

What to Do

1 Help students trim the curved edges of the plastic-foam tray so that a flat section remains. Then ask them to lightly sketch a simple picture of the person they chose. When they are satisfied with their sketch, ask students to retrace it, pressing firmly to leave a deep imprint.

2 Using tempera (in a color that contrasts with white), show students how to ink the brayer and roll it evenly over the imprinted image. Then ask students to invert the plastic foam and lightly press it to the 4-by-6-inch paper, being careful not to slide it, so they make a clear impression on the paper.

3 Ask students to carefully remove the paper from the plastic foam, pulling gently from one corner. Some students may need more than one try to make a print that they are pleased with. Once they have, ask them to repeat the process to create two more prints.

4 As students wait for their prints to dry, have them look through the magazines and photos to find and clip images of objects that might belong to the person they admire.

5 When their prints dry, instruct students to cut around one of the portraits and glue it to the 9-by-12-inch construction paper. Ask students to print the singular possessive of their hero's name above the picture.

29

Parts of Speech

6 Invite students to glue the clipped pictures, or to draw their own, around the portrait print.

7 Ask students to trim around their second and third prints. Invite them to glue their prints to the 12-by-18-inch paper. This time, ask students to write the plural possessive of their hero's name below their prints. In the example shown here, three students decided to work together to create their plural possessive portrait since they had all done images of their grandmothers.

8 Encourage students to paste or draw additional pictures around these plural possessive portraits. After discussing the different pictures, wrap up by reviewing the difference between singular and plural possessives.

Extended Learning

Students may enjoy creating Impressive Possessive Portraits as part of informational science or social studies reports. If you were doing a unit on scientists or presidents, for example, you might create a class portrait collection. Using a large sheet of mural paper, students can affix their portrait prints and pictures. This project could be called "Scientists' Work" or "Our Presidents' Profiles."

Ways to Share

- Impressive Possessive Portraits make a powerful hallway display, especially when students embellish the prints with sentences that use the singular and plural possessive forms (for instance, "A rhino's hide is thick and strong" or "Tigers' stripes hide them from prey").

Parts of Speech

Preposition Scenes

Students make colorful dioramas and manipulative characters to move about the scene in this hands-on lesson on prepositions.

Materials

- shoe box or small rectangular box
- scissors
- construction paper or construction-paper scraps
- pencil
- crayons
- markers
- tape
- glue
- clay
- notebook paper

Advance Preparation

- Ask students to bring a shoe box or other small box from home.

- Before starting, you may want to make and model a Preposition Scene. Using construction paper and markers, create a scene with grass, bushes, the sky, a tree, a creek, a small bridge, and a doghouse. Add a clay animal, like a dog, to move about the scene. (See What to Do on page 32 and the photo of the completed activity above.)

- Demonstrate prepositions by manipulating the dog *inside* the doghouse, *around* the tree, *through* the bushes, and so on. Write the actions on the chalkboard, underlining the prepositional phrases.

Parts of Speech

Getting Started

After discussing this part of speech, ask the class to brainstorm a list of prepositions and prepositional phrases. Point out that prepositions get us where we need to go—*on* the bus, *down* the street, *back* to school.

What to Do

1 Divide the class into pairs and ask partners to decide on an animal or character to create. Explain that they should mold the animal from clay.

2 Invite students to use construction paper, crayons, and markers to create the objects and background for their Preposition Scenes. Show them how to make a little lip at the bottom of the objects (a tree, a bush, a bridge) by folding the paper back about a quarter-inch. Then ask students to glue or tape this object to the inside bottom of the box.

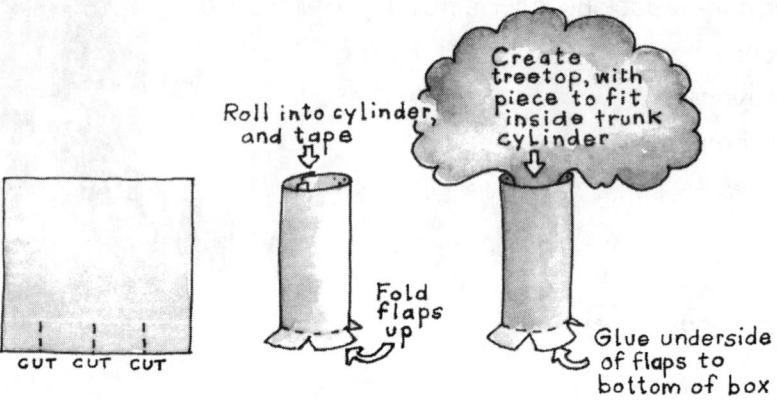

3 Invite partners to take turns manipulating the animal or character around the different parts of the setting. While one moves the figure, ask the other partner to write down the prepositional phrases being demonstrated. When they finish, ask partners to exchange roles.

4 Have students work alone to write a paragraph about the animal or character, using prepositional phrases to describe their actions. Remind them to underline the prepositional phrases.

Extended Learning

Try applying Preposition Scenes to help students demonstrate a historical event in a social studies lesson.

Ways to Share

- Invite students to share their scenes and paragraphs with the rest of the class. Follow up with a group discussion on the effectiveness of prepositions in descriptive writing.

- Working in groups of three, students can videotape the figure's actions in the scene. Guide one member to shoot with the video camera while another manipulates the figure. The third member of the group reads the descriptive paragraph as voice-over narration.

Parts of Speech

ACTIVITY 13

Homophone Cubes

Students construct Homophone Cubes to focus on the different spellings and definitions of these tricky words.

Materials

- Homophone Cube pattern (one for every student)
- markers
- scissors
- glue or tape
- notebook paper

Getting Started

Review homophones with students, writing down a few examples on the chalkboard. Then divide the class into small groups to brainstorm lists of homophones. Have groups share their lists.

Homophone Cube Pattern

34

What to Do

1 Distribute copies of the Homophone Cube pattern (page 34) to your students. Have them write a different homophone on each face of their cube before they assemble it.

2 Invite students to assemble their cubes by folding along the dotted lines, and securing the sides with glue or tape.

3 Invite students to share their homophone cubes. Then ask them to write the shared homophones and their meanings on a separate sheet of paper. Remind them to double-check the spelling.

Extended Learning

Students might also enjoy making homophone wheels. Ask students to cut two same-sized circles from a sheet of construction paper. On one of the circles, cut out a window shaped like a pie slice. On the second circle, ask students to draw lines that divide the circle into sections the same size as the window on the first circle. Invite students to write a pair of homophones in each of these sections. Then have them attach these two circles with a brass fastener so that the circle with the window is on top. Students can share their homophone wheels and refer to them again and again to help build their vocabulary.

Ways to Share

- For a cooperative learning strategy, invite small groups of students to play a game in which they toss a homophone cube around. When a student catches the cube, he or she must make up a sentence that uses that homophone correctly.

Parts of Speech

35

Parts of Speech

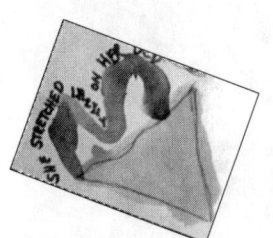

Animated Adverbs

Overview

Students create animated line drawings to illustrate adverbs.

Materials

- 1 sheet of 12" x 18" white construction paper
- tempera paint
- paintbrushes
- pencil
- fine-point marker

Getting Started

You might want to show the class examples of Wassily Kandinsky's artwork, which is often characterized by flowing abstract shapes, kinetic lines, and bursts of expressive color. Choose some of the simpler lines, patterns, and shapes, and draw them on the chalkboard. Explain that this is the kind of art they will be making.

What to Do

1. Work with students to brainstorm a list of adverbs. You can either do this as a class or have students work in small groups.

Parts of Speech

2 When students have compiled a substantial list of adverbs, invite them to use tempera paint in any color(s) to make six or seven shapes on the white construction paper, holding it horizontally. When their shapes have dried, ask students to select different colors and to paint directional and expressive lines on top of the shapes.

3 Encourage them to use the "action" of the lines to inspire adverb choices. For example, a zigzag line might remind a student of the adverb *energetically*; a gently swirling line might remind a student of the adverb *lazily*.

4 Once students have selected adverbs for each line drawing, ask them to use pencil to write sentences using these adverbs around the shapes. Then have them highlight the adverb by retracing it with fine-point marker.

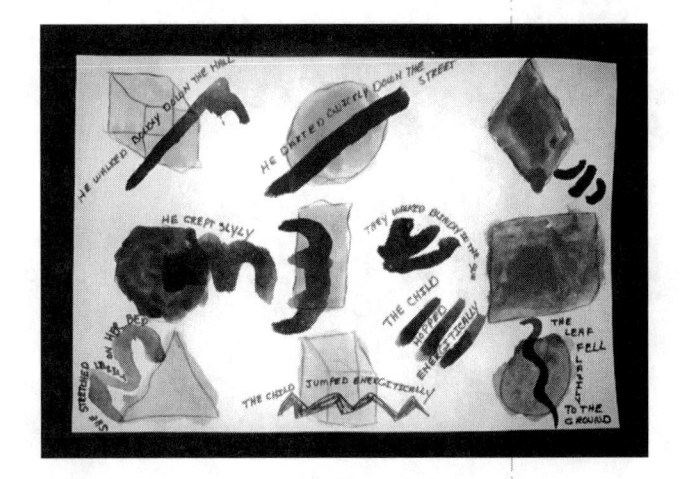

Extended Learning

Ask students to write a short story or paragraph that uses plenty of adverbs. Then invite them to repeat the painting activity, this time spacing the shapes to accommodate the sentences and designing the lines to illustrate their adverbs. When the paintings are dry, invite students to add the sentences from their paragraph or story. Again, ask them to accentuate the adverbs.

Ways to Share

- Mat inspired adverb paintings on a slightly larger sheet of construction paper (14" x 20") in a contrasting color. Display the work in the hallway or other shared space.

- You might want to add students' adverb artwork to their portfolios along with a writing sample to see if the activity increased their use of adverbs and descriptive language.

Parts of Speech

ACTIVITY 15

Antonym & Synonym Puzzle Pieces

Overview

Students make colorful puzzle pieces to help them visualize antonyms and synonyms.

Materials

- 9" x 12" construction paper in various colors (6 sheets per student)
- 1 sheet of 12" x 18" black (or white) construction paper
- ruler
- scissors
- pencil
- markers
- glue

Getting Started

Together with the class, brainstorm pairs of antonyms and synonyms and list them on the chalkboard in two columns headed "Antonyms" and "Synonyms." Be sure to introduce some new words that relate (as synonyms or antonyms) to words that students already know. For instance, in response to the synonyms *big/huge*, you might introduce *massive*. As you do, write *huge/massive* on the chalkboard, as it is helpful for students to see a new word paired with a familiar one.

Parts of Speech

What to Do

1 Instruct students to cut each sheet of colored construction paper into 4-by-8-inch rectangles. (The 9-by-12-inch paper will yield three rectangles per sheet.) If necessary, guide them in using rulers and pencils to do this.

2 Ask students to couple about half the rectangles in pairs of different colors and half in pairs of the same color.

3 Instruct students to hold their rectangles vertically and to bisect the different-colored pairs simultaneously in creative puzzle-piece ways so that the patterns are identical. When they finish, ask them to pair the different colors of the same cut.

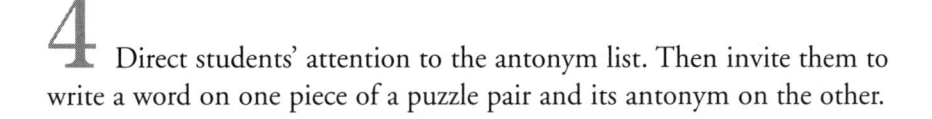

4 Direct students' attention to the antonym list. Then invite them to write a word on one piece of a puzzle pair and its antonym on the other.

5 Ask students to repeat this process with the pairs of rectangles that are the same color. When they finish, invite them to label the pairs with synonyms.

6 When their antonym and synonym pieces are labeled, invite students to select their three favorite pairs and glue them to the construction paper. Then ask that everyone put her or his remaining puzzle pieces into a box, where they can be mixed up for a game of "Match the Antonyms and Synonyms."

Extended Learning

Invite pairs of students to trade antonym and synonym pieces and to write sentences that use the synonyms and antonyms they receive from each other.

Ways to Share

- Display the mounted antonym and synonym pieces around the classroom or even in the hallway.

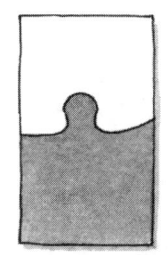

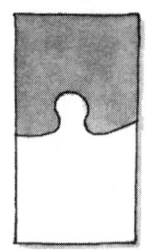

Reading Skills

ACTIVITY 16

Main-Idea Flowerpot

Overview

Students make construction paper potted plants to identify and isolate the main idea and specific details of a paragraph.

Materials

- 1 sheet of 9" x 12" colored construction paper
- 5" x 7" piece of construction paper in colors that will contrast with above
- 1" x 6" strips of green construction paper (4 per student)
- assorted construction paper scraps in various colors
- scissors
- glue
- pencil
- ruler
- black marker

Advance Preparation

Precut the construction paper to the dimensions shown in the Materials list. Optional: If you have adequate computer capabilities, you might want to guide students in producing the main idea and details electronically. They could then cut and paste the printout text on their Main-Idea Flowerpots. This approach not only provides computer practice but also fits nicely into the collage.

40

Reading Skills

Getting Started

Review finding the main idea and identifying the important details of a paragraph. Model this process with the class. Then divide the class into small groups and assign them another paragraph for cooperative reading and summation. Ask students to agree on the main idea as well as three or four supporting details. Remind them to highlight or jot down the information they learn in their cooperative groups.

What to Do

1 Invite students to cut out a flowerpot from the 5-by-7-inch construction paper, using the full height of the paper. Then instruct them to glue the flowerpot on the 9-by-12-inch paper. Explain that they should align the bottom of the pot with the bottom of the paper, which should be positioned vertically.

2 Ask students to write the main idea on the flowerpot in black marker. They may want to use a pencil and ruler to lightly draw handwriting lines.

3 Invite students to write each of the supporting details on a different "stem" of 1-by-6-inch green construction paper, leaving enough room at the top to attach a flower. Then ask them to arrange the stems at the top of the pot.

4 Ask students to design and cut flowers from the construction paper scraps and glue a flower to the top of each stem.

5 Next, students should glue their supporting-detail flowers to the paper at the top of the stems. When the flowers are firmly affixed, encourage students to design and cut leaves to glue to the stems.

Reading Skills

6 Wrap up by asking students to write the paragraph's title or topic at the top of the paper and their name at the bottom.

Extended Learning

- To help students keep their comprehension skills sharp, periodically apply this activity to information in newspaper or magazine articles or to various science and social studies lessons.

- Encourage students to design another whole-part metaphor to replace the flowerpot and stems. Some examples include main-idea hands (with the palm for the main idea and the fingers for details) and main-idea trees.

Ways to Share

- Students can save a Main-Idea Flowerpot each month to include in their assessment portfolio.

- Create a beautiful school "garden" by displaying Main-Idea Flowerpots on the wall outside the classroom.

ACTIVITY 17

Nonfiction Kites

Overview

Nonfiction Kites encourage students to find and visualize the main idea and essential details in their nonfiction reading. By illustrating a kite with the big picture and adorning its tail with pictured details, your students will see their reading skills soar.

Materials

- photocopy of a textbook page (one copy per student)
- highlighters in a few colors
- 1 sheet of 12" x 18" white or light-colored construction paper
- ruler
- pencil
- scissors
- crayons
- 3" x 5" index cards (6–8 per student)
- hole punch
- yarn
- tape

Getting Started

- Help students select a challenging lesson from one of their nonfiction texts. Ask them to read one or two pages and hold up a finger for every main idea or related detail they read. This will help students recognize the number of details represented. Explain that locating and visualizing details helps readers understand and remember what they read.

- Then guide students in highlighting the important information in the text.

- Now select a different text page and photocopy it for this activity.

Reading Skills

What to Do

1 Divide the class into groups of three or four, and ask students to read through the selected text to find the main topic and highlight the important details. Then ask students to return to their seats to work individually.

2 Ask students to hold the 12-by-18-inch paper vertically and to use their ruler and pencil to draw a big diamond, which will be the body of their kite. When they finish drawing the diamond, invite them to cut it out.

3 Invite students to write and illustrate their topic sentence on their diamond cutout. Encourage them to take up as much of the space as they can so that they get a big picture.

4 Help students punch holes in the bottom of the main-topic kite and the top center of each index card. Now ask students to use the blank side of the index cards to draw a picture of each of the supporting details. Explain that they should use a separate index card for each detail. On the ruled side of each index card, ask students to summarize the illustrated detail in a few words.

5 Then assist them in threading and knotting the appropriate length of yarn through the kite and detail cards to complete the project.

Extended Learning

- Try making Nonfiction Kites an integral part of your students' informational reports.
- Text-driven kites are a great way to reinforce difficult grammar lessons. The kite might show a sentence (in color), for example, while the detail cards isolate and identify its parts of speech.

Ways to Share

- Display Nonfiction Kites in the classroom as a reminder to students to identify and visualize details when reading.

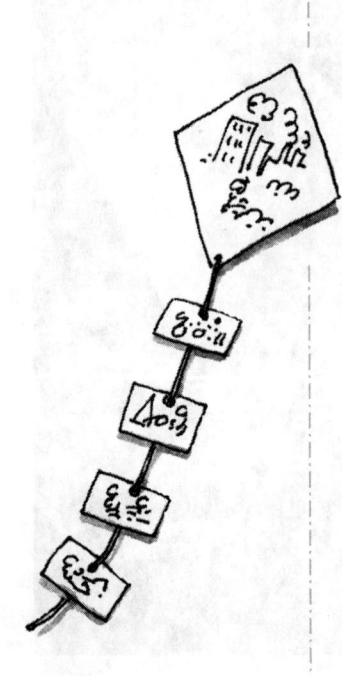

ACTIVITY 18

Story Ads

Overview

Students practice their comprehension skills and learn to prioritize and organize information by creating an ad for a story they've read.

Materials

- assorted magazines
- scrap paper or notebook paper
- 8 1/2" x 11" white paper
- ruler
- pencil
- construction paper scraps in a variety of colors
- scissors
- glue
- crayons
- markers

Getting Started

- Divide the class in half and assign a different story to each half.

- Before they begin reading, discuss the importance of seeking out the main ideas and essential details of a story as they read.

- Ask students to jot down these important story points, and explain that they will use them to create an advertisement that aims to entice other students to read the story.

What to Do

1 After students from both halves of the class finish reading, ask them to consider their notes and review the main idea and outstanding details of their assigned story.

Reading Skills

2 When students are satisfied that they have grasped the main idea and essential details, ask them to study the magazines to compare a variety of advertisements.

3 Divide each half into groups of three or four, and ask groups to brainstorm ways to use print, drawings, color, and space to create intriguing advertisements of their own. Urge students to design their ad on notebook or scrap paper.

4 Explain that students should hold the 8 1/2-by-11-inch paper vertically. Then encourage them to use the ruler to draw lines for various lettering sizes. Invite them to cut letters from the construction paper scraps to display the title of the story and to use markers for the key phrases or ideas.

5 Have students use a collage of appropriate pictures from magazines to augment their own illustration.

6 Pair students who have worked on different stories, and ask them to exchange ads. Encourage discussion on the effectiveness of the Story Ads. Remember to point out that story elements like character, setting, and plot are important things to note in assessing the ads' success.

Extended Learning

If your school has computers, you might want to bring technology into the Story Ad activity. A word processing program will enhance the ads by providing an array of text fonts and sizes. Story Ads would also benefit from a multimedia program like Power Point. You could extend this comprehension activity by videotaping students' presentations.

Ways to Share

- Post Story Ads in the library to encourage students from other classes to read the story and practice their reading skills.

Reading Skills

ACTIVITY 19

Story Genre Paintings

Overview

Students create genre paintings to illustrate their understanding of the difference between realism and fantasy.

Materials

- pictures of realistic and unrealistic still life painting
- 12" x 18" white or light-colored construction paper (two sheets per student)
- construction paper scraps in a variety of colors
- scissors
- glue
- pencil
- crayons (regular and glitter)
- markers
- watercolor paints

Advance Preparation

Compile examples of still life paintings from a variety of art schools, both realistic and unrealistic. Cubism will probably strike students as the most obviously unrealistic work that still has a discernible image. Artists to keep your eye out for include Bruegel, Rubens, and Rembrandt (realism); Courbet, Cezanne, and Matisse (impressionism and fauvism); Picasso, Braque, and Gris (cubism); and Dali (surrealism).

Getting Started

Discuss the differences between the realistic and the fantastic in fiction, movies, and television. Cite various stories the class has read, and ask students to classify each as an example of realism, fantasy, or a combination of both. Explain to children that comparing a story's setting, characters, and events with their own experiences is a good way to determine if it is realistic or fantastic. Then pick a couple of brief stories or excerpts that exemplify these two genres, and ask students to read them aloud and discuss them in class.

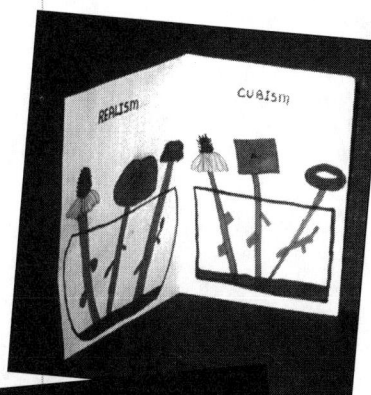

Reading Skills

What to Do

1 Show and discuss realistic still lifes with students, explaining ways used to make an object look real (like scale, shape, and color). Then ask them to fold one sheet of construction paper in half and use the left side to draw and color an object (from a painting or from the classroom) as realistically as possible.

2 Introduce unrealistic still lifes to the class, particularly cubist work. Invite students to cut construction paper scraps and glue them to the paper's right side to depict the same object they made on the left in an unrealistic—or fantastic—way. (Some students may prefer the less fragmented style of Matisse or Cezanne.)

3 Together with students, isolate and review images from the realistic selection they read in class.

4 Ask students to fold the second sheet of construction paper (as in step 1), and invite them to use pencil, paper, and watercolors to paint one of the realistic images discussed in step 3.

5 Now review and discuss the fantasy selection read in class. Discuss what makes this story a fantasy, and ask students to help you single out the elements and images that are not like real life.

6 On the right side of the paper, invite students to depict one or more images from the fantastic story as unrealistically as they'd like. Encourage them to use as many materials as they need. When they finish, ask students to use a marker to title each side of their artwork.

Ways to Share

- Display Story Genre Paintings in the classroom or hallway. You might want to ask students to include a brief written explanation along with the display.

Reading Skills

ACTIVITY 20

Cause-and-Effect Inventions

Overview

Students create inventions to extend their understanding of the concept of cause and effect.

> Name: The Adventure Car 2,000 & 1 By: Jeff Doan
>
> Problem Solves: It is electric powered and uses no gas. If it has a flat tire, it can fly to help. If it falls in water, it can swim to shore. It has a code box as a door opener. The headlights are waterproof and the car is sealed so water can't get in. If you are late to a meeting. It bends your stuck in traffic, it can fly to your meeting. The body so it can parallel park even if it is a 1 cm space. The body of the car is like rubber so if you wreck, it will go back to how it was and the other person's car will be just fine like it was a dream. The windows are bullet proof so if a rock or bullet has hit the window, it won't break. The airbags have a sencer so it fits perfectly for the person in that seat, that will make it so kids 1 and up to adult can sit in the front. The hubcaps are built in the tire so the hubcap won't fall off unless the tire comes off too. The car has a hidden radar so you can tell it where to go and the hidden radar will spot the place and park where you want it to. The car's radar can see in color so you can go to sleep while it gets you to where you want it to take you. The car comes with a control so if your lost you can type in a number and the car will find you in less than 10 sec. I think this car will help the Anviorment because it doesn't use gas. I think it would be $10,000.

Materials

- scratch paper
- pencil
- 1 sheet of 8 1/2" x 11" white paper
- ruler
- fine-point marker

Getting Started

- Begin with a discussion of cause and effect, citing examples from stories the class has recently read. Ask children to contribute instances of outcomes that result from a character's actions.

- Then divide the class into groups of four or five, and encourage students to work cooperatively to brainstorm various examples of cause-and-effect relationships both from literature and their own lives.

- Discuss how inventors work with cause-and-effect relationships to make their inventions work.

Reading Skills

What to Do

1 Ask students to design a new vehicle that is powered by the energy of one person's movement combined with the energy of the wind, sun, or water. Explain that they should use the scratch paper to work out their design.

2 Once they have finished developing their design, invite students to use a pencil to draw the vehicle on the white paper, tracing over their drawing in fine-point marker for boldness and contrast.

3 On the back of the paper, ask students to name and write about their invention, explaining how it works and what effects it will have on people's lives.

Extended Learning

If possible, encourage students to use a computer to do the written part of the activity. After printing out the explanation of the invention, they can glue it to the back of the illustration. Students might also work in cooperative groups to create a three-dimensional model of the invention of their choice.

Ways to Share

- Cause-and-Effect Inventions make an interesting display for a science room or area.

- Invite students to combine their Cause-and-Effect Inventions with a story that predicts what their life might be like in the future.

Reading Skills

ACTIVITY 21

Double-Meaning Scenes

Overview

In Double-Meaning Scenes, students use collage to illustrate different meanings of the same word. This activity also features a movable part: a paper-strip slide-out sentence that describes the scene by using the chosen word in both of its senses.

Materials

- 1" x 6" paper strip
- fine-point marker
- pencil
- ruler
- construction paper scraps in a variety of colors
- scissors
- glue
- 1 sheet of 12" x 18" white or light colored construction paper

Advance Preparation

Although you can instruct students to cut the 1-by-6-inch paper strips, you might want to precut them to save time.

Getting Started

Invite students to help you brainstorm a list of words that have more than one meaning (like *park, bat, mouse, light, pop, cool,* and *hail*). Then let everyone take a turn making up a sentence that uses both meanings of the same word—for instance, "Park the car in the park." List students' favorites on the chalkboard, keeping in mind that the sentences should describe an image that students can illustrate.

Reading Skills

What to Do

1 Invite students to select one of the double-meaning sentences you listed on the chalkboard or one of their own to write on their movable sentence strip with the fine-point marker.

> Park the car in the park.

2 Have students use a pencil, a ruler, and the construction paper scraps to design the objects, details, and scene described in the sentence. Then let students cut out their scene elements.

3 Ask students to begin the collage by gluing the largest picture piece to the 12-by-18-inch construction paper. Guide them in gluing the piece along only its top and bottom. The sentence strip will tuck behind this piece so it can be slid in and out. Once the strip is in place, students can continue composing their Double-Meaning Scenes.

4 When they finish, ask students to slide the sentence strip out from the picture, read the sentence, and identify the different meanings of the word.

Extended Learning

Invite students to work in cooperative groups to do this activity on mural paper with several multiple-meaning words and several accompanying slide-out sentences.

Ways to Share

- In a paired sharing activity, ask partners to exchange their double-meaning sentences with each other. Once they are familiar with the definitions, encourage students to add these words to their personal dictionaries.

Reading Skills

ACTIVITY 22

Past-Tense Silhouettes

Overview

Language arts, history, and art come together as students go back in time to create Past-Tense Silhouettes.

Materials

- pictures of people from various historical periods
- 1 sheet of 12" x 18" white construction paper
- tape
- lamp or overhead projector
- pencil
- fine-point marker
- crayons
- notebook paper

Getting Started

- Collect pictures (preferably headshots) of people from various historical periods, like Colonial America, Medieval Europe, and Ancient Egypt.

- Then begin by reviewing verb tenses with students, zeroing in on the present and past tenses. You might write some sentences on the chalkboard and ask students to help you change them from the present to the past and vice versa. Be sure to use some sentences that feature irregular verbs.

- Move from a discussion of the past tense to a discussion of historical periods. Ask students which of the people from the pictured periods interest them and why.

Reading Skills

What to Do

1 Encourage students to talk about themselves—their interests, their pastimes, their goals. Then invite them to write self-portrait paragraphs, making sure to use verbs in the present tense.

2 For each student, tape a sheet of construction paper in a vertical position to a bare wall and ask him or her to stand before it in profile. Then shine a light from an overhead projector (or a strong lamp) on the student's face, and, using pencil, trace the silhouette on the paper.

3 Invite students to select one of the historical periods you shared in the Getting Started section. Then have them add facial features, hairstyle and head wear of the period to their own silhouettes.

4 Encourage students to add details of the historical setting to the background of their picture. For example, an Ancient Egyptian portrait might have pyramids, the sphinx, or the Nile River in the background.

5 Divide the class into groups of four, and ask them to collaborate on predicting what daily life was like during the historical period that each group member has chosen. Then, with the self-portrait paragraph as a guide, encourage students to use the past tense to write about what their lives might have been like at that time.

Extended Learning

You may want to apply Past-Tense Silhouettes to historical periods that students learn about in social studies. These silhouettes can serve as powerful tools in reinforcing lessons on state history, national history, or world history.

Ways to Share

- Past-Tense Silhouettes and their accompanying paragraphs make vibrant and informative hallway displays.

Reading Skills

ACTIVITY 23

Cartoon Quotations

Overview

Cartoon Quotations enable students to create characters and practice writing dialogue complete with quotation marks and related punctuation.

A fish in a hat waltzed into an ice cream store.
"This is very good for a fish!" he thought.
"$1.00" said the clerk.
"I am still hungry!" said the fish as he walked away.

Materials

- several published comic strips
- 1 sheet of 9" x 12" white drawing paper
- pens or markers
- scissors
- notebook paper

Advance Preparation

Clip and collect several appropriate comic strips from newspapers. Then photocopy them so that you can distribute one copy of each to your students.

Getting Started

Share the comic strips with students, and discuss what they have in common. Ask students to pay attention to what characters say to each other and which words are included in the speech balloons. Then explain that dialogue is presented differently in prose writing. Using character names and dialogue from the cartoons, model some examples on the chalkboard. Be sure to include action and description. Point out that dialogue must be enclosed in quotation marks and that it is followed by punctuation.

What to Do

1 Ask students to fold the drawing paper into three horizontal panels.

Reading Skills

2 Next have students fold the paper vertically so that it is divided into 9 frames, each approximately three by four inches.

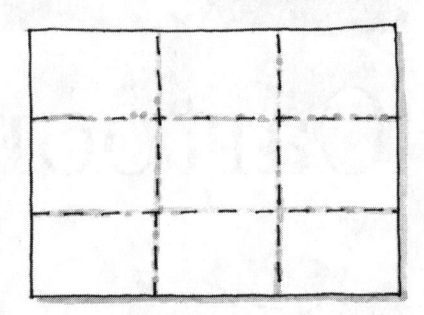

3 Invite students to draw a short cartoon in the top three panels, including dialogue between the different characters. (Students with longer ideas can use more frames.) Explain that the dialogue should be enclosed in speech balloons, which are like the quotation marks of comic strips.

4 Ask students to cut off any unused frames from the paper. These can be saved for another cartoon.

5 Invite students to study their cartoons and retell what is happening in a one- or two-paragraph story written on notebook paper. Remind them to enclose the dialogue in quotation marks.

6 Encourage students to share their cartoons and stories with each other.

Extended Learning

Combine usage practice with comprehension practice by encouraging students to summarize a short story with a Cartoon Quotation. Or, for a curricular link to social studies, invite students to use Cartoon Quotations to retell historical events.

Ways to Share

- Combine students' cartoons in a comics page. Then copy the students' stories on the back or facing page, and send it home to parents as part of a class newspaper.

Reading Skills

ACTIVITY 24

Base-Word House

Overview

Students build Base-Word Houses to build their vocabulary.

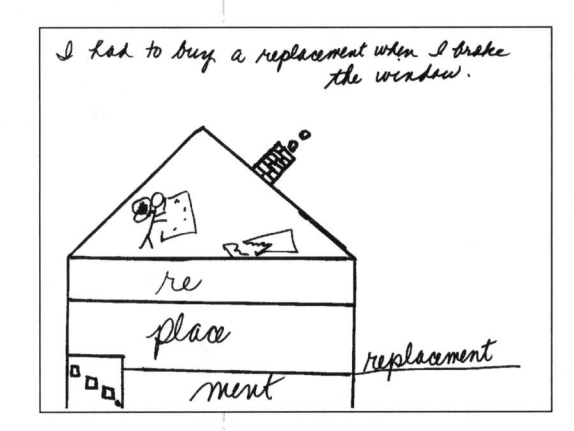

Materials

- 8 1/2" x 11" paper (10–12 sheets per student)
- pencil
- ruler
- fine-point marker
- crayons or colored fine-point markers

Advance Preparation

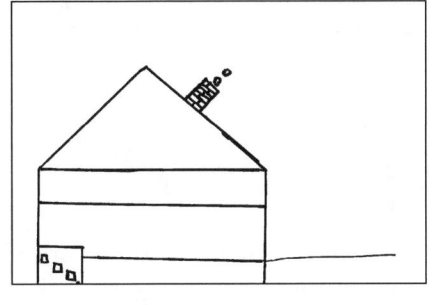

On 8 1/2" x 11" paper positioned horizontally, draw a simple cross-section of a two-story house that includes a basement and an attic. Draw the house toward the left side of the paper. Indicate the ground by making a line at the bottom of the main floor on both sides of the house. On the right side, this line will serve as a place to write a word. (You may want to photocopy the drawing to distribute to students.)

Getting Started

Review word parts (prefix, base, suffix) with students. You might want to draw a four-column chart on the chalkboard with the headings "Word," "Prefix," "Base," and "Suffix." Then list words in the left column, breaking them into their parts in the following three columns. Explain to students that words don't always have prefixes and suffixes and provide them with some examples.

57

Reading Skills

What to Do

1 After sharing the house diagram with students, ask them to use a ruler and a pencil to draw several of their own. Refer to the lower level of the house (that is, the ground floor) as the base floor. once they've drawn the houses correctly they may go over the pencil lines in ink.

2 Have students choose a word from the chart and print (in pencil) the prefix of the word in the top floor, the base in the base level (or ground floor), and the suffix in the basement. On the ground line to the right of the house, students can write the complete word.

3 Now ask students to make up a sentence that uses the word, and instruct them to write the sentence across the top of the paper.

4 Invite students to illustrate the sentence in the attic of the house. If some students make up a sentence that does not lend itself to illustration, ask them to try again. They'll catch on in no time.

5 Encourage students to repeat this process with several words to increase their ability to visualize word parts.

Extended Learning

Apply the diagram for Base-Word Houses to the study of verb tenses, particularly those of irregular verbs. On the ground line, ask students to write the infinitive of the verb. Then instruct them to use the basement for the past tense, the ground floor for the present, and the second floor for the future. In the attic, students can draw a picture that expresses the action of the verb. Across the top of the paper, they can write a sentence that uses the verb.

Ways to Share

- Students can compile their Base-Word Houses in a book that has a table of contents listing all the words. Encourage them to continue adding pages to the book throughout the year, which will help them to break down longer and more difficult words. Base-word books are great to share with classmates.

Reading Skills

ACTIVITY 25

Word-Root Trees

Overview

Students discover just how useful word roots can be when trying to determine the meaning of new words they encounter.

Materials

- 1 sheet of 9" x 12" white or light-colored construction paper
- pencil
- fine-point markers in three colors
- construction paper scraps
- scissors
- glue

Advance Preparation

Try to come up with a word root and four to six related words for each student in your class.

Getting Started

Discuss word roots with students, along with some information on word origins. Point out that many words have the same root. (Examples include *advent, adventurer, invent,* and *prevent*, which all derive from the root *vent*.) Explain that once you learn the meaning of the root (and of some prefixes and suffixes), it is possible to determine the meanings of many other related words. Work with students to complete a chart of roots and their related words.

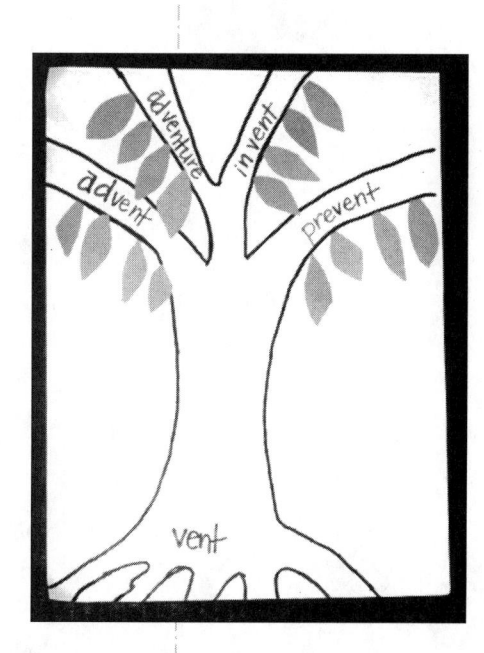

Reading Skills

What to Do

1 Invite students to draw a large tree with 4–6 big branches that touch the top and sides of the paper, and 4–6 short roots cut off at the bottom of the paper. Guide them to fill as much of the paper as possible. Then, ask them to depict the ground just above the roots by drawing a line on either side of the trunk.

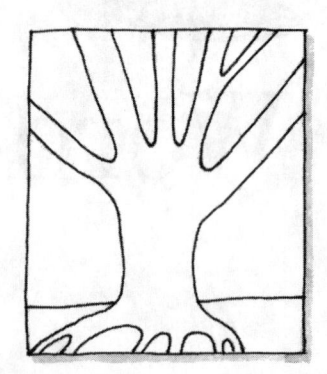

2 From the brainstormed list, assign each student a different word root to illustrate. Have students write their word root in the root area of the tree using a specific color marker.

3 Ask students to write a word that uses the root in each of the branches. For emphasis, have students write the root in the same color as below, and write the rest of the word in a contrasting color.

4 Invite students to cut leaves from the construction paper scraps and glue them to the branches and/or the ground in their picture.

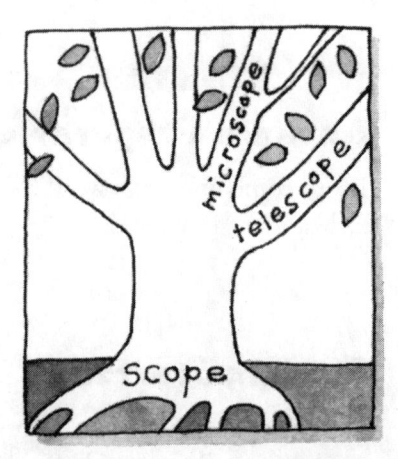

Ways to Share

- Display Word-Root Trees in a hallway or classroom exhibition titled "A Forest of Words."

- Compile an ongoing "Classroots" book by keeping a three-ring binder of Word-Root Trees. On the back of the trees, students can include a definition or a sentence that uses each word. Arrange the root trees in alphabetical order, and encourage students to add to the book whenever they learn a new word root. As "Classroots" grows, it should prove a fruitful resource.

Spelling Skills

ACTIVITY 26

Illustrated Definitions

Overview

Students make pictures out of words to help them remember word spellings and definitions.

Materials

- illustrated dictionary
- 8 1/2" x 11" white paper (3–6 sheets per student)
- notebook paper
- pencil
- crayons or colored pencils
- stapler

Advance Preparation

Compile a list of about 20 spelling words, half of which should be nouns or words that readily lend themselves to illustration.

Getting Started

Using an illustrated dictionary or glossary, discuss with students the various parts of an entry (bold-faced word, pronunciation in brackets or parentheses, abbreviation for part of speech, and definition). Point out the illustrations to students, and explain that the pictures usually illustrate nouns. Review that a noun is a person, place, thing, or idea. Then write the 20-word spelling list on the chalkboard, and invite students to become dictionary illustrators.

What to Do

1 Ask students to study the spelling list and choose the words that would be easiest to illustrate.

Spelling Skills

2 Instruct students to fold a few sheets of the paper into quarters. When they unfold them, explain that they should hold their paper horizontally.

3 Invite students to print a spelling word at the bottom of each section and then illustrate the word to define it. Explain that they should label any parts of the picture that require explanation, just as is done in a dictionary.

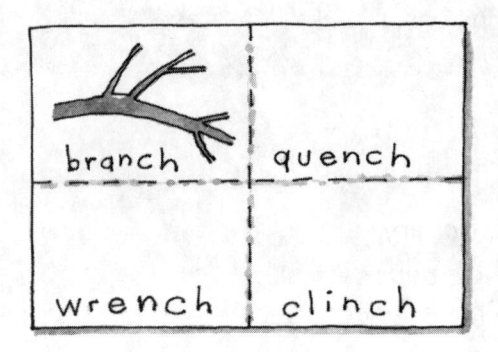

4 Ask students to use notebook paper to write complete dictionary definitions for the rest of the spelling list.

5 Have students staple both parts of the assignment together before they turn it in.

Extended Learning

Students can extend their illustrated words into illustrated sentences that they write across the bottom of a 9-by-12-inch sheet of drawing paper. In a frame around the sides and top of the paper, ask students to print the spelling words over and over. Then invite them to use the rest of the space to illustrate the sentence.

Ways to Share

- Create a Spelling Corner in the classroom and display students' Illustrated Definitions there. Encourage students to add their own pictured words to the Spelling Corner whenever the illustration urge grabs them.

Activity 27

Rough-Tough Words

Overview

Rough-Tough Words give students a hand in rating the spelling difficulty of the words they encounter every day. Students rank words as green (easy), yellow (causing some hesitation), and red (rough-tough) and then write the red words on paper placed over sandpaper. The resulting textural effect creates an appropriate image of the word—and sticks in students' memory.

Materials

- 1 sheet of 4" x 8 1/2" coarse sandpaper
- 4" x 8 1/2" blank newsprint (several sheets per student)
- red crayons
- stapler

Note: sandpaper sheets (and newsprint) of comparable dimension will work just as well.

Advance Preparation

Precut the newsprint to the dimension of the sandpaper.

Getting Started

After making a spelling list, discuss with students the relative spelling difficulty of various words. Explain that they can use the word *green* to refer to words that are easy to spell because they possess a direct sound-letter correlation. They can use *yellow* to rate words that make them slow down and think of a spelling rule or recall a nonphonetic letter group. *Red* is for rough-tough words, the ones students find really hard to spell. Invite each student to select six to eight red words that he or she finds particularly challenging.

Spelling Skills

What to Do

1 For each red word, students can place a sheet of newsprint on top of the sandpaper and write the word in red crayon, sounding the word out as they spell it.

2 Ask each student to repeat this procedure for each tough word that he or she encounters.

3 Invite students to share and study their Rough-Tough Words.

4 If you'd like, you can give a spelling test and see how accurately the Rough-Tough Words are spelled.

Extended Learning

Invite students to create a traffic light spelling list. Have them draw a traffic light and write red, yellow, and green words in the appropriate circles.

Ways to Share

- Post Rough-Tough Words around the classroom, and encourage students to add or remove words throughout the year.

Spelling Skills

ACTIVITY 28

Palindrome Pictures

Overview

In this activity, students identify—or invent—palindromes and accentuate them with symmetrical art.

Materials

- 8 1/2" x 11" white paper (2 sheets per student)
- pencil
- scissors
- markers of various colors
- fine-point black marker

Getting Started

- Lead students in a discovery and discussion of palindromes by writing one on the chalkboard and asking what is special about the word.

- Begin a palindrome list (*mom, dad, kook, level, Anna, Hannah, radar,* and *race car*), and see if students can add to it. You might post the collection of palindromes, allowing a few days for students to find more.

- When the list is done, draw a few simple symmetrical pictures (a heart, a star, a butterfly) on the chalkboard. Then explain to students that they can work with symmetry in words and pictures.

What to Do

1 Instruct students to hold their papers horizontally and then fold them in half vertically.

65

Spelling Skills

2 Invite students to use a pencil to draw the outline of a butterfly or other symmetrical shape that is clearly divided down the middle by the vertical fold.

3 Ask students to refold the paper so they can see a half of the picture on either side of the paper. Then ask them to cut out the shape and color their picture.

4 Now invite students to choose a palindrome and print its letters in black marker across the cutout shape.

Extended Learning

Invite students to increase the shape-word link of Palindrome Pictures by making a symmetrical cutout of the thing the palindrome describes. For instance, they might draw one half of a race car on a folded sheet of paper and then cut it out. When they unfold the paper, they're ready to decorate and label the picture.

Ways to Share

- Encourage students to take their Palindrome Pictures home and share them with parents. Ask them to see if their parents can help them come up with more palindromes.

- Share palindromic phrases with students, and encourage them to make Palindrome Pictures that illustrate the phrases. Here are a few to start with: "Madam, I'm Adam," "Sit on a potato pan, Otis," and "Poor Dan is in a droop."

ACTIVITY 29

Capital-Idea Pictures

Overview

Students use self-assessment and art to overcome stumbling blocks in cursive handwriting.

Materials

- 1 sheet of 9" x 12" white or light-colored construction paper
- ruler
- pencil
- fine-point black marker
- crayons or markers

Getting Started

- Display cursive formation of capitals, discussing techniques for making difficult letters. Then give students a standard cursive alphabet of capital letters.

- Review handwriting strategies, emphasizing key aspects of letters that students can focus on to compare their own writing with the standard form.

- Have students write the 26 capitals and assist each student in assessing the letters he or she should work on. Then form practice groups of four or five, and invite students to follow up that work with guided practice at the chalkboard.

What to Do

1 Ask students to use the ruler and the pencil to make a 1-inch frame on the construction paper.

Handwriting Skills

2 Have students use their pencil and ruler again to lightly trace handwriting lines for writing one large letter, about an inch from the top and bottom frame lines.

3 Tell each student to choose the letter that gives him or her the most difficulty; then invite everyone to write his or her chosen letter within the lines in the middle of the paper.

4 Ask students to trace the correctly formed capital letter several times to make it look bold and thick enough to carry off its height.

5 In the one-inch frame around the letter, students can draw and color pictures of things that begin with their practice letter.

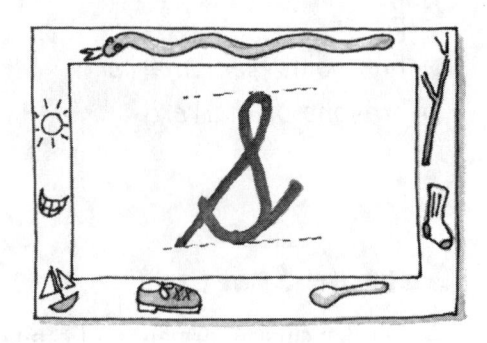

Extended Learning

Invite students to practice their capitals by writing poetry based on their Capital-Idea Pictures. Ask them to start each line of verse with the plural form of one of the pictured things. For example, a poem based on a capital-idea C might begin, "Cats eat mice/Cars go fast/Candles never burn twice/Clocks say the day passed . . ." Be sure to remind students that poetry doesn't have to rhyme.

Ways to Share

- Encourage your students to work together to make a Capital-Idea Picture for each letter of the alphabet and post them above or below the classroom alphabet.

Handwriting Skills

ACTIVITY 30

Painted Quotations

Overview

Students adorn watercolor paintings with their best cursive script.

Materials

- notebook paper
- pencil
- 4 1-gallon containers of water (total for whole class)
- 8-ounce plastic or plastic-foam cups
- watercolors and paintbrushes
- 1 sheet of 9" x 12" white construction paper
- pen or fine-point black marker

Advance Preparation

Find some examples of impressionist painting such as the work of Monet, Renoir, or Manet. Then compile a collection of about 10 to 12 simple quotations and proverbs and write them on the chalkboard.

Getting Started

- Share the impressionistic prints with students, pointing out that the shapes and forms are not painted with sharp edges or precise lines.

- Then share the various quotations and proverbs, and invite students to explain what the sayings mean. After discussing the sayings, write a few on the board in cursive.

What to Do

1 Invite each student to choose a favorite saying or quotation to inspire their painting.

Handwriting Skills

2 Have students write their quotation in cursive on a sheet of notebook paper. Ask them to practice any letters they have trouble writing.

3 Distribute an 8-ounce cup of water to each student, and ask students to use a paintbrush to lightly wet the paper.

4 Have students hold the construction paper horizontally, and invite them to begin painting their pictures. Encourage them to let some colors run on the wet paper. Remind them that they can use as many colors as they like.

5 When their paintings are dry, ask students to lightly pencil handwriting lines across the part of the painting where they want the saying to appear.

6 Invite students to write their quotation in pencil, retracing it in pen or fine-point marker only when the handwriting is correct.

Extended Learning

Combine handwriting practice with spelling skills by inviting students to make painted sentences. Instead of displaying a saying on their paintings, students write a sentence that contains two or three words they spelled incorrectly on a spelling test or homework assignment. This could also serve as a springboard for a calligraphy activity.

Ways to Share

- Mat or frame finished Painted Quotations and display them as inspirational art throughout the school.

- Encourage students to make additional Painted Quotations to decorate their home or to use as gifts for family and friends.

Handwriting Skills

ACTIVITY 31

Signature Silhouettes

Overview

Students practice writing their signatures within the lines of their silhouetted profiles. Beyond providing handwriting practice, this activity will delight students with its visually inventive and personalized results.

Materials

- masking tape
- 1 sheet of 12" x 18" white construction paper
- lamp or overhead projector
- pencil
- fine-point black marker
- **Optional:** crayons or markers

Advance Preparation

You may want to make silhouettes of student profiles in advance to allow more time for students to practice their handwriting and fill their Signature Silhouettes.

Getting Started

Discuss with students the importance of their signature and how writing one's name well is something to take pride in. Go on to discuss positive character traits, and comment on all your students' admirable characteristics. Encourage them to acknowledge good qualities in their fellow students. Finally, offer instruction and encourage practice in the cursive writing of student signatures.

Handwriting Skills

What to Do

1 For each student, lightly tape a sheet of construction paper to a bare wall and ask him or her to stand before it in profile. Then shine a light from an overhead projector (or a strong lamp) on the student's face, and, using pencil, trace the silhouette on the paper.

2 Ask students to use a fine-point marker to retrace their silhouette.

3 Have students draw ribbonlike bands within the silhouette by making sets of double lines.

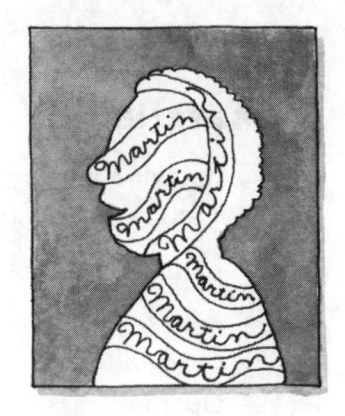

4 Now invite students to write their signature several times within and/or between the bands.

5 The background can remain blank, or you can invite students to fill it with various colors or illustrations of their interests or hobbies.

Extended Learning

To enhance their Signature Silhouettes and extend handwriting practice, invite students to fill the spaces between their signatures with strengths or positive qualities that you or their fellow students have shared with them. Or you might encourage students to accompany a Signature Silhouette with a brief autobiography or an essay that expresses their dreams and goals.

Ways to Share

- Display Signature Silhouettes across classroom walls.
- Encourage students to give Signature Silhouettes as gifts to family members.

Handwriting Skills

ACTIVITY 32

Good Signs

Overview

Students strengthen their communication skills, including organization of ideas, prioritization of information, and presentation, by creating posters to announce upcoming school events.

Materials

- notebook paper
- pencil
- 1 sheet of 12" x 18" construction paper
- ruler
- markers or crayons

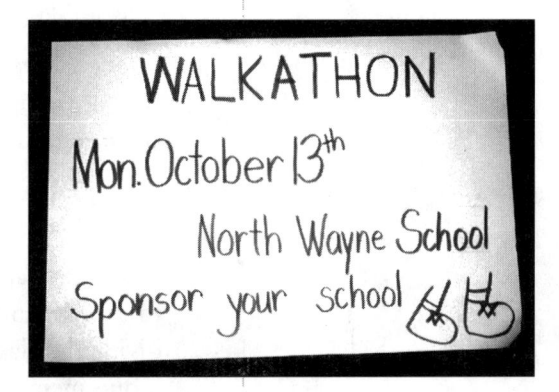

Advance Preparation

Collect examples of student-made signs from around the school. If none are available, collect flyers or take pictures of signs that are displayed in the community.

Getting Started

Use the collected signs to start a discussion on what makes a sign effective. Then divide the class into small groups, and ask them to discuss which signs had the greatest impact on them. Students can work as a class to explore the common elements of those signs and list them on the chalkboard. Explain that these skills (prioritizing information, using catchy language, having an attractive presentation) can be applied to the sign they're about to make.

Handwriting Skills

What to Do

1 Enlist students' help in determining the important information that needs to be included in the sign. List the information on the chalkboard alongside the criteria for effective signs.

2 On notebook paper, students can number information in order of priority. Encourage them to discuss where the most important information should be placed on their sign.

3 Invite students to make a rough design of the sign on notebook paper to help plan spacing and size of letters. Encourage them to give consideration to effective wording, the use of color, and possible use of illustration. Once they are happy with their sketch, have them make their sign on the construction paper.

4 After allowing students ample time to experiment and finish their signs, divide the class into small groups. Ask group members to give feedback on one anothers' signs.

Ways to Share

- Encourage students who enjoy making signs to advertise their sign-making abilities, letting the school staff know that they are available to make signs for various events.

- Have a sign-making contest, and allow the entire student body to vote on entries displayed in the hallways.

Poetry

ACTIVITY 33

Paper-Animal Haiku

Overview

Students compose Paper-Animal Haikus to develop their descriptive writing and creative expression.

This is my monkey. It thinks it's really funny, But it's really not.

Materials

- wildlife books and encyclopedias
- 1 cardboard tube from bathroom tissue or paper towel roll
- scissors
- glue (preferably with glue brushes)
- construction paper in various colors
- fine-point marker
- scratch paper
- pencil

Advance Preparation

Construct a paper animal from a small cardboard tube and construction paper (see What to Do below) to share with your students. You might also want to precut most of the paper-towel tubes to the length of a bathroom tissue-tube. (Leave a few long ones to accommodate the occasional dachshund or centipede.)

Getting Started

Share your paper animal with students and then embark on a discussion of poetry as a means of expressing things in a succinct and intense way. Demonstrate a haiku on the chalkboard, perhaps one about the animal you shared. Point out the three-line form and five-seven-five syllable pattern of haiku. Finally, remind students that when they write their haiku, they can express any feelings that they or their animal might have.

What to Do

1 Invite students to think of an animal they would like to make and write about. Encourage students to refer to the wildlife books if they need to look at a picture to get started.

75

Poetry

2 Ask students to use scissors and glue to cover the cardboard tube with construction paper that matches the animal's color. (Point out that rolling the paper around the tube is a good way to gauge the size to precut. Brushing the tube with glue before attaching the paper also works well.)

3 Encourage students to use construction paper scraps to form the head, legs (and arms), and tails of their animal. Then ask them to glue the parts to the animal's body.

4 Invite students to add details (facial features and markings, like stripes or spots) in contrasting colors of construction paper scraps.

5 Now invite students to write a haiku about their animal on a white or light-colored construction paper scrap. When they're done, ask them to use pencil to draw a cloud around the words. Then instruct them to cut out the haiku along the pencil line. Ask students to attach the haiku cloud behind the animal's head.

Extended Learning

Divide the class in half, and invite each of the students in one half to write a haiku from the point of view of an animal—without using the name of the animal. (For instance, "I am black and white/I can eat tons of bamboo/I look cuddly too.") Encourage the other half of the class to guess the animal. Then have the two groups exchange roles.

Ways to Share

- Work with the whole class to make a haiku zoo. Use a large section of mural paper, crayons, markers, and construction paper to create a nature scene with trees, grass, water, and sky. Then invite each student to glue her or his Paper-Animal Haiku to the scene.

Poetry

ACTIVITY 34

Cartoon Limerick Strips

Overview

Students use their imaginations and the magic of poetry's rhythm and rhyme to create humorous limerick cartoon strips.

Materials

- 36" strip of adding machine tape
- pencil
- fine-point marker
- colored pencils or crayons
- 1 sheet of 9" x 12" black or dark-colored construct
- Exacto™ knife
- ruler

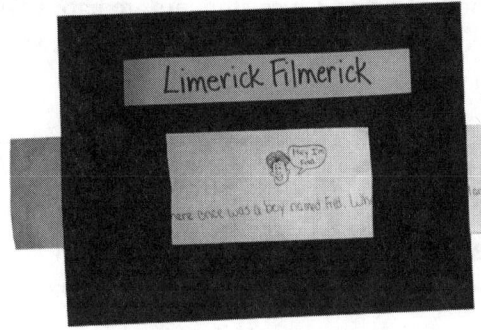

Advance Preparation

Compile a collection of about five or six limericks and photocopy them for your students. Then, using an Exacto™ knife, preslice one sheet of construction paper per student. To do this, position the paper horizontally and use a straightedge as a guide to make a vertical slit starting 3 inches from the top left edge of the paper. Make an equivalent slit on the right side.

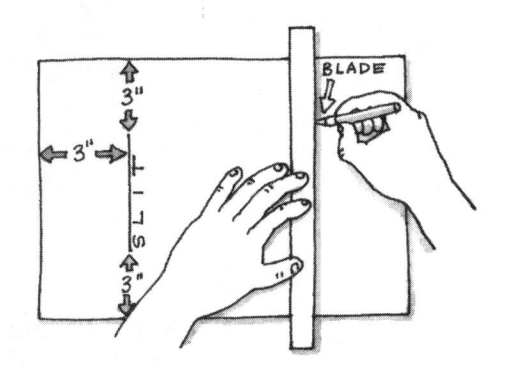

Getting Started

Divide the class into small groups and ask them to read the limericks, paying attention to their meter and rhyme scheme. Encourage students to share their discoveries with the class. After they become familiar with the form, you might want to write a class limerick together. Start by writing the first line on the chalkboard (for instance, "A young girl who came from the east"), and then ask students to contribute ideas for the rest. When creating their own limericks, students can work alone or in pairs.

77

Poetry

What to Do

1 When they are done composing their limericks, ask students to write them in pencil along the lower edge of their adding machine tape.

> There once was a man named Fred

2 Invite students to illustrate each line of the limerick in cartoon style above the text. Once students are happy with their limericks and accompanying illustrations, they can trace over them using a fine-point marker.

3 When they finish their cartoon limerick strips, invite students to thread the strip through the pre-slit construction paper, revealing one line at a time.

4 Ask students to write the title of their limerick at the top of the paper along with their name.

Extended Learning

For a curricular link between language arts and social studies, encourage students to write limericks that describe historical figures and events. Or make a bridge to science by challenging students to write limericks about inventors and their discoveries.

Ways to Share

- Ask students to rewrite their limericks in standard form (that is, in five stacked lines) in their very best handwriting. Then bind the poems into a class limerick book for students to read again and again.

- Include a limerick from the Cartoon Limerick Strips in a weekly class newsletter.

ACTIVITY 35

Color-Coded Poems

Overview

Students create color-coded poems to learn more about meter and rhyme.

Materials

- notebook paper
- pencil
- 1 sheet of 9" x 12" white or light-colored construction paper
- highlighters in various colors
- crayons or markers in various colors

Advance Preparation

Collect examples of brief poems (or poem stanzas) with simple meter and rhyme scheme. Then photocopy and distribute them to the class.

Getting Started

Discuss the different poems with students. Lead them in an observation of the rhyme scheme and meter of each. Point out where the beats are by vocally stressing certain syllables, and explain that this syllable pattern helps give a poem its rhythm. Then focus on which lines rhyme, reminding students that these poems were planned by the poets to fit this pattern. Finally, invite students to choose a poem that has a pattern they'd like to use in a poem of their own.

What to Do

1. Ask students to count the number of syllables in each line of the poem and illustrate this pattern by writing a blank line for each syllable on a sheet of paper. Explain that each line of the poem should be represented by a corresponding line of blanks.

Poetry

79

Poetry

2 Ask students to highlight the last syllable in each line, color-coding the highlights to designate the lines that need to rhyme with each other.

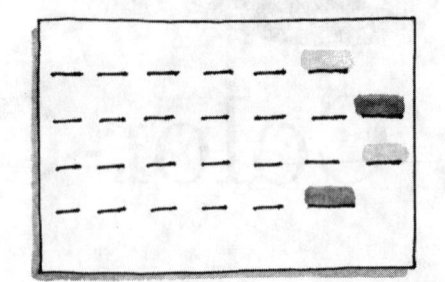

3 Invite students to experiment with rhymes and syllables, either with a partner or on their own, as they write the lines of their poem.

4 Ask students to double-check or let their partners double-check the rhyme scheme and number of syllables in each line.

5 Ask students to use pencil to copy their poem neatly onto the construction paper. When they approve of its layout, invite them to retrace the words in marker and highlight the rhymes. Then encourage them to illustrate their poem.

Extended Learning

Invite students to color-code the lyrics of one of their favorite songs.

Ways to Share

- Bind a collection of student poems together in a class poetry book and offer the collection to the school library.

- Invite students to keep a collection of their own poems in a blank book. They can start by copying the poem they wrote for this activity. Encourage them to save the book and continue to add poems to it.

- Encourage students to submit their poems for possible publication in children's magazines or other outlets, such as the local newspaper.